AF578560

My Mindset:

The key to a successful life

By

Larry. S. Daniel

Copyright @2022 Larry. S. Daniel

All rights reserved

Table of content

Introduction

Change your perspective, transform your life. It sounds so simple, yet many of us tell ourselves that we dont have enough time to learn something new or that its too late to change careers. We feel we cant, so we dont, which leads to a self-fulfilling prophecy when we live with these restrictive thoughts. Imagine what we could accomplish if we lived by the mottos "I can" and "I will" instead!

My belief is that our thoughts have tremendous influence over how we behave and feel in daily life. Thinking positively begins with imagining solutions rather than dwelling on obstacles. Great success in life is largely an attitude issue. Instead of the other way around, how we think has a direct impact on the results we produce. Our decisions and behaviors are determined by the thoughts we have.
Our thought processes are reflected in our actions, routines, and even emotions. This implies that we are all entirely accountable for

the lives we lead. Were in command, whether it works or not. Because of this, leaders have been talking a lot about success attitude.

First, let me ask you: what does success mean to you?

Im certain that at least a portion of it would consist of both financial success and individual and professional accomplishments. You are the only one who can determine when you have achieved the level of success you were striving for, whatever that may mean to you.

You would probably agree that there are numerous facets to success and that having a certain degree or income level is not sufficient on its own. Feeling satisfied with who you are and the decisions youre making is a necessary component of true success and prosperity. And that indicates that thought mastery is where it starts.

Chapter 1

What is mindset?

A mindset is a way of looking at things. Our attitudes act as a set of glasses through which we view the outside world. Additionally, if the prescription is off, everything appears hazy, exactly like with traditional glasses. In life, we will battle unnecessarily if our perspective is off.

Because they have the power to significantly affect how we think and feel about ourselves and the world around us, we need to be careful about who and what we let into our brains.

Optimistic Or Pessimistic Attitude

Your mentality is a conglomeration of ideas and convictions that directs the way you think. Additionally, the way you think, feel, and act are all influenced by the way you think. Your mental attitude affects how you interpret the world and how you interpret yourself. Our mentality is important.

Whether we have an optimistic or pessimistic outlook, it will affect us, frequently inadvertently.
For instance, our perspective may increase our propensity to give up in the face of adversity or to take chances.

Its crucial to concentrate on what you want since doing so will help you locate it in your life.

When we know exactly what we want, our minds are free to consider opportunities and solutions that will get us there.

Modern technology has demonstrated that this pessimism is no longer necessary, but because our minds are hardwired to detect negativity, it can be challenging to shift our perspective.
Which mentality would you select then?

- **Why is mindset important in life?**

Image of a human silhouette explaining the value of mindset in life

It goes without saying that having a positive outlook on life is essential for leading a contented and happy existence. Many people are unaware of the fact that your thinking is actually fairly resistant, but if you want to improve your life, you can change it.

Recognize The Value Of Mindset

It is impossible to stress how crucial mentality is because it is the foundation of everything. Success and pleasure in life are impossible without a good outlook.

So why is adopting the proper mindset so crucial?

Because it can affect whether or not your life is successful.

A optimistic outlook will support you in achieving your goals and upholding a healthy lifestyle, whereas a pessimistic outlook will result in negative outcomes. It is obvious that having a positive outlook on life is necessary for happiness and success.

Chapter 2

How Does Mindset Affect Success?

A success mentality encourages strategic thinking, boosts self-assurance, and equips you to respond appropriately when things dont go according to plan. Its what permits us to experience life fully and without looking back.

Here are just a few advantages that changing your mindset can help you accomplish:
Despite your reservations and worries, act.
Consider issues as obstacles to be overcome.
Intense circumstances, maintain composure.
Be able to handle pressure and tension.
Take initiative and make decisions.
Adopting a success mentality has several advantages, including fostering a healthy sense of self-worth, thinking positively, giving any event a healthy purpose, igniting motivation, dealing with adversity with assurance, and more.

The mindset we approach things with is our mental attitude. It is a collection of ideas, presumptions, and convictions. What inspires us, maintains our attention, and gives us power is the attitude for success

- **Why Mindset Is the Key to Success?**

The difference between those who achieve and those who dont is mindset. You must develop your own if youre serious about succeeding in any aspect of your life. You can alter your behavior by altering your way of thinking.

Results change when action does.In other words, what you think about, you become.As soon as you begin to alter your perspective, you will also alter your conduct.
In theory, it could seem simple, but dont be deceived by the seeming ease. Its not the kind of thing that succeeds overnight. With the proper perspective, there are, however, methods and resources that can and will assist you in succeeding. The good news is that you already possess all the necessary resources in you.

Although the phrase "Change your mentality, change your life" may seem simple, many of us place restrictions on ourselves. We argue that it is too late to start a new career or that we lack the time or resources to learn a new talent.
Our world is a result of these limiting ideas.Imagine what we could accomplish if we lived by the mottos "I can" and "I will" instead!

Here is a straightforward fact:

There is no need for more time. There are exactly 24 hours in a day for everyone of us. To be prosperous, you dont need to have more money. Start where you are, as most people do. You dont need to be exceptionally talented or skilled. If there is a desire, it can be developed. All you need to do to change your thinking from failure to success is to be willing to do it. The main reason to adopt a success mentality is the tremendous influence that our thoughts have on how we live our daily lives.
In actuality, thinking and perspective are inseparable. How we interpret information and view the world around us is inevitably

influenced by our underlying beliefs, attitudes, and prejudices. The likelihood of forming a successful perspective and achieving long-term success increases with positivity.

Chapter 3

How to change your mindset for success?

An illustration of a journal with the words "Money attitude on how to improve your mindset for success" is shown.
One of the most crucial things you can do for yourself if you want to succeed is to alter your thinking.

Your mindset will dictate how you approach issues, how you react to mistakes and setbacks, and how much effort you put into whatever it is that youre doing.

The phases in this process are intended to assist you in seeing the importance of what youre doing to yourself. Once you have reached this realization, it will be simpler to alter your perspective and succeed.

- **Search for trends**

You must first recognize the thought pattern you need to alter in order to shift your attitude for success.

This might be difficult if youre unsure about what you want to change, this could be challenging. But once a pattern is recognized, breaking it can be a crucial step toward success in life and personal development.

Once a mindset has been discovered, changing it is not always simple, but doing so is frequently essential for success and personal development.

- **Remain Inspired**

It takes drive and attention to change your thinking; it is not an easy process. These traits are essential for doing anything, including shifting your thinking.

You can alter your perspective and succeed if you have the correct tools and attitude.
And although it may be challenging, the effort is unquestionably worthwhile

- **Confront Your Dread**

You must first conquer your fears in order to transform your thinking for success.

Although it could appear difficult, this is an important phase in the procedure.

This will take a lot of people, including me, the longest to complete.

You can continue with the subsequent steps of altering your mentality and succeeding once you have faced and overcome your anxieties. Do not forget that it is difficult yet worthwhile!

- **Modify Your Inner Dialogue (And Those Around You)**

Success depends on having an optimistic outlook.
Its crucial to start your day off right and to have a pleasant outlook all day. This entails speaking positively and supportively to yourself.

This will keep you inspired and committed to achieving your objectives.

This entails switching up your mantra and inner dialogue as frequently as necessary to stay motivated and on track. Additionally, you should be conscious of your own unique triggers and make an effort to alter your mentality prior to these occurrences.
If you want to alter your thinking for success, it is crucial to surround yourself with like-minded others. This will serve to motivate you and support your new beliefs. It is also beneficial to talk to yourself positively.

- **Action Plan**

Making a plan of action is the next step after identifying a negative thought pattern. Its crucial to alter your thinking in addition to taking action—in fact, they go hand in hand!

Youll need perseverance and motivation, just like with any other goal you might have in life, such as losing weight or learning a new skill.

If at first you dont succeed, try again, as the saying goes.
Although it can be difficult, changing your perspective is definitely doable with time and effort.

So keep moving forward till your objectives are attained!

Chapter 4

How do you develop a successful mindset?

Possessing the proper mindset—a growth mindset—is the key to success.

Here are 8 success mindsets that help you achieve success:

The 8 Success Mindsets

Learn these eight mindsets for success and pay attention to the changes they make in your life to make sure youre constantly in the appropriate frame of mind to be successful.

If you want to live an incredible life, keep in mind that you are in control and have all you need to do it.

1. A mindset of self-acceptance

Everything begins within of you. Youll be able to adapt and develop beyond your wildest dreams the better you learn to know yourself.

The simplest way to describe it is in this well-known phrase from an anonymous author:

"Life dies if an egg is cracked by an external force, but life begins if the egg is broken by an internal force. Everything great always starts inside.

- **Learning About Oneself**

With all the peculiarities, differences, advantages, and difficulties, we are who we are. Successful people are always conscious of their actions and emotions during difficult circumstances.
There wont be any learning or growth in your life if there are no failures or challenging situations. Just remember that pain is not necessary. Although successful people may fight to reach their objectives, they wont suffer because they understand the difference between the two. Success and failure are differentiated by this distinction.

- **The Secret to Lifes Success**

Do you realize that the secret to success is your mindset? Discover how to improve your success mentality with Lifehacks insider tips!
Putting faith in your gut

Knowing when to act is crucial, as is having faith in your instincts to guide your decision-making so that it is perfectly in line with your goal. Your best ally can be your inner voice. Having confidence in oneself will enable you to overcome obstacles.

When faced with a task, using encouraging self-talk helps keep you motivated and focused.

- **Be honest in your communication.**

Discover the purpose of your speech.
Talk in the second person to yourself. It improves both your capacity for and actual performance.
Speak aloud. It increases your capacity to remember information and learn.
Having faith in your own abilities, abilities, skills, and drive.
Given that achievement takes time, self-belief and patience go hand in hand. You become less focused and more self-conscious when you are impatient. Recognize your inner fortitude and have faith that they will help you when you need it.

- **Acknowledging Your Passion**

Your route to success will be straightforward and simpler since your passion will enable you to have pleasure. Spend some time discovering your passion. It will support you when youre struggling.

You have that inner desire to generate better results when you are passionate about what you do.

"A significant portion of your life will be devoted to your profession, and the only way to feel completely fulfilled is to produce what you consider to be outstanding work. And doing outstanding work is only possible if you enjoy what you do.

- **Being self-compassionate**

It all comes down to admitting your mistakes and then forgiving yourself. It will be easier for you to let go of mistakes and move on if you practice self-compassion.

Saying "no" more frequently is a fantastic place to start. Its a method of enforcing your limits, and boundaries are for ensuring that your demands and priorities are met.

2. **Setting Goals Mindset**

Knowing what you desire will help you stay motivated to get it. The objective must be interesting and difficult.

Setting goals correctly is crucial since it will enable you to achieve your objectives without worrying about the deadline. It wont alter you if it doesnt challenge you. Aim high and keep going until you achieve your goals.

Your objective is your goal, and the more clearly you can see it, the more focused youll be on getting there. Eliminating distractions and moving forward with your goals will be made possible by living with a clear intention.
You are already positioning yourself for success if you are clear and specific about what you want to accomplish in life. Youll perform considerably better than most people whose

goals in life are unclear. It will be simple for you to develop a goal-setting attitude if you possess the sound wisdom of emotional and personal fulfillment.

Its time for you to take control of your life and consciously work toward your specific objective in order to achieve the fantastic success you desire.

3. A Learning Attitude

You must pursue progress if you want to be successful. We can bring about change if we have faith in it. Everything in your life will begin to reflect your newfound confidence in your ability to succeed.

When discussing how learning leads to growth, there are a few things I want to make clear. You are still learning even if you are having difficulty. You can learn from every setback, and every lesson you acquire advances your development.

No one can assist you if you dont want to learn. Nobody can stop you from learning if you are committed to it.

- **Have no fear of failing**

The fear of failure prevents many people from achieving great things. However, that can be resolved by picking up new abilities, becoming more proficient at specific chores, and creating fresh strategies.

Consider each mistake you make as a means to learn from failure. Taking a chance can be intimidating at times, but keep in mind that you will learn and develop more the more times you fail.

- **Learn New Skills**

Learning new talents might be very difficult, but you must keep in mind that it takes time. As soon as we begin practicing a particular talent, we are never as good as we can be at it. To perfect it requires effort and patience.

Put less pressure on yourself whenever you start learning a new skill. Instead, accept that you will experience difficulties. Simply concentrate on your learning process, beginning small and then developing your talents from there. Over time, progress will become apparent, which will boost your learning confidence.

- **Be Inquiring**

A excellent quality that may be fostered for a success mentality is curiosity. Your mind will be exposed to a wide range of possibilities through curiosity, which focuses on what can be learned. Its a terrific opportunity to work on letting go of a particular style of thinking.

Try to tame your inner critic, and act against your anxieties to foster curiosity. Start by asking how, why, and why not.

A passion for knowledge should be a lifelong pursuit because it can never be satisfied. The secret to looking beyond whats in front of you, learning what you are genuinely capable of, and maintaining a growth mindset is to have an unending supply of curiosity.

- **Leave your comfort zone.**

Leaving your comfort zone will be a terrific learning experience that will help you grow. By doing so, you will challenge your prior experiences and push yourself to new heights. Failure to step beyond of ones comfort zone is a recipe for failure. Stop letting it be you. Keep in mind that a learning mindset embraces the learning process, which includes learning from errors, failures, setbacks, and challenging situations. Therefore, even after failing, you must ask yourself what you are learning.

By doing this, youll be better equipped to spot opportunities for improvement and be less likely to interpret failure as setbacks and blunders. But the point here isnt to over-optimize and overlook errors. It involves identifying lessons that can be drawn from anything.

4. The Challenge of Mindset

You will be challenged by choosing a challenge. It will push you past your comfort zone and force you to change and broaden your perspective.

It requires courage and determination to overcome obstacles.But being brave does not imply being fearless. It indicates that you are prepared to confront your anxieties and proceed.

Like a muscle, courage may get stronger with use. Youll always learn something new if you push yourself. You could definitely fail. But in the process, youll discover something about yourself that you otherwise wouldnt have, such as what you can do differently the next time to ensure you perform better.
You can fast advance your talents with a mindset change since youll start approaching every new task with joy and confidence rather than avoidance and dread.

Being successful entails standing out from the crowd, which is just what you must do to achieve success. You will achieve the same outcomes as most people if you follow their lead.

Have the confidence to make a difference by challenging yourself, being unique, and being yourself. You have to step outside your comfort zone if you want to be different. You have to keep challenging yourself to reach new heights. To later reap bigger advantages, you must do the uncomfortable thing.

5. **Concentration**

Losing focus and letting procrastination take over is one of the worst mistakes you can make on the road to success. Being focused and disciplined is not always simple, despite how vital it is. The best strategy is to remain present and focus on everything that is happening right now.

We all know that procrastination prevents progress and that distractions waste time. The link between goals and success is discipline, and a mindset of focus creates that link.
Success rarely occurs overnight, and even when it does, it usually took more than that. A focused mindset is helpful in this situation. You can maintain focus by making a long-term

commitment to achieving your goals. Your capacity to concentrate on the long-term effects is thus one of the essential success mindsets.

Keep your vision in mind and keep working toward it. You may keep your behaviors in line and your drive high by having a clear vision.

6. **A positive outlook**

One of the first steps to developing a success mentality is to concentrate on the good things. Youll become more fulfilled in addition to happier and more successful as a result. How can that be accomplished?

Because positivity spreads, its important to feed your mind with positive information every day and surround yourself with people who can help you live your best life. Positivity will start to direct your actions once you acquire it. Success comes your way when you have a successful attitude. To become your happiest, most contented self, you just need to make a few minor changes to your way of thinking.

Your life will be greatly impacted by your decision to adopt a positive outlook and a good attitude. Give yourself justifications for why you can and should pursue your goals rather than justifications for why you cant or shouldnt. Keep in mind that happiness never stems from outside conditions.

There is undoubtedly some good in everything, even though everything may not be excellent. Your efforts to succeed will be substantially enhanced if you concentrate on those good qualities.

7. **A spirit of abundance**

People who are successful consistently think they have ample chances to succeed in life. You wont have to worry about things not being enough if you practice having an abundant mentality.

The abundant mindset holds that there is enough prosperity for everyone and that everyone benefits. You can break free from constraints by

realizing that there is more than enough success to go around. Its a terrific habit to form and uphold to accept other peoples accomplishments because it will open up additional doors for success and advancement.
When you think there is plenty and an abundance of opportunities all around you, you will begin looking for them. This is the time when fresh opportunities present themselves and greater abundance comes your way in a variety of forms.

8. **Festive Attitude**

Indulge in success. If its difficult for you, its time to develop and maintain this habit. It will not only help you get over your worries, but it will also open your eyes to new paths, chances, and prospects for even more development.

This is your chance to change if you enjoy celebrating your success but often feel jealous of others accomplishments.

You can get rid of bitterness and animosity by celebrating other peoples achievements. It also enables you to concentrate on your accomplishments that are constructive.

Because you are unable to obtain the things you despise, resentment destroys your prospects of achievement. So, practice celebrating both your own and other peoples triumphs.

Feel elated for those that succeeded going forward, even if they are your rivals. Tell yourself you can accomplish it because others have done it. They just demonstrated to you that it is feasible to accomplish something, somehow.

The mindset of celebration will be supported by cultivating an attitude of thankfulness because it emphasizes growth rather than lack. Finding a bright side is not naive. T is sage advice that you ought to follow religiously.

Thinking like a winner is another excellent technique for developing a celebration mindset. Too many people mistakenly believe they are focused on winning when, in reality, they are more concerned with avoiding defeat. There is a significant difference because, when you concentrate on winning, you are worried about taking chances and moving outside of your comfort zone.

If youre having trouble, consider what a winner would do. Get the confidence to say "try me" rather than whining and asking "why me."

Conclusion

The art of mindset is undoubtedly a work in progress. You must practice it until it becomes a habit that you cant live without. Every big success takes our commitment, perseverance, and capacity to grow. Without modifications, advancement would not be possible.

To improve your life, you must first transform yourself, beginning with acquiring a successful mindset. Create new habits for better results starting today and watch as your life transforms before your very eyes.
You must be able to trust yourself and have faith in your abilities if you want to succeed. Success is something you build, not something that just happens.

You now have the information and resources needed to alter your perspective. Your time has come. You have the power. Its time to put those eight success attitudes into practice step-by-step so you can get the money, health, and happiness you want. Decide consciously to control your thinking and strive for higher success this year and in the future. Your mentality is the secret to living a great life. Learn how to achieve your maximum potential by adopting a success attitude.

www.ingramcontent.com/pod-product-compliance
Lightning Source LLC
LaVergne TN
LVHW020536160826
845677LV00015B/4082

* 9 7 9 8 8 4 7 3 3 3 1 3 9 *